Division of Beat

*A Breath Impulse Method For
Intermediate Band Classes*

BOOK 1B

Supplemental Material

By

**Harry H. Haines
Music Department Chairman
West Texas State University
Canyon, Texas**

And

**J. R. McEntyre
Coordinator of Music
Odessa Public Schools
Odessa, Texas**

Contributing Editor

Tom C. Rhodes

SLIDE POSITION CHART

TROMBONE

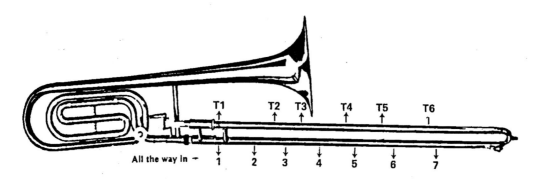

The number of the position for each note is given in the chart below.
T indicates F attachment trigger.

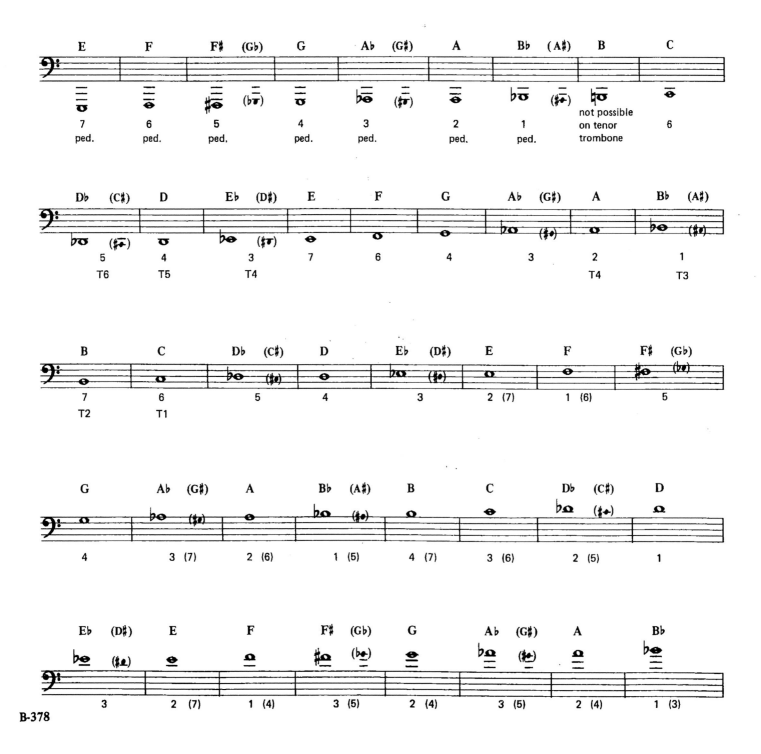

BAND WARM-UPS

To Be Added Gradually Throughout the Book

1 Two Breath Impulses Per Beat 4 breath impulses on each tone of the chromatic scale.

2 Three Breath Impulses Per Beat 6 breath impulses on each tone of the chromatic scale.

3 Four Breath Impulses Per Beat 8 breath impulses on each tone of the scale.

4 Six Breath Impulses Per Beat 12 breath impulses on each tone of the scale.

5 Eight-Five-One Slur Practice slowly! Work for smooth even slurs.

6 Flexibility Exercise Practice slowly at first, then push for greater speed.

7 Five-Note Slur Practice slowly (suggest ♩=50). Keep the airstream flowing smoothly! It's the *quality* of the slur that is most important.

8 Flexibility Exercise Practice slowly at first. If necessary, play each note as a ♪, then as a ♫

LESSON 1

1 Scale Partners

2 Duet Part

3 Chalumeau Etude

4 Slurring's The Thing

5 Chromatic Etude

Watch Out!

6 Amazing Grace

7 Grandfather's Clock

8 Little Canon

PART 1

PART 2

PART 3

LESSON 2
Concert F Lesson

1 **Scale Duo**

2 **Duet Part**

3 **Clarinets the Same (As lesson one)**

4 **Chromatic Exercise**

Watch Out!

5 **Skip To My Lou**

6 **Same Tune**

7 **Tom And Jerry Duet**

8 **Duet Part**

B-378

LESSON 3

1 "The" Scale

2 Duet Part

3 Clarinets Right Hand Down

4 Chromatic Challenge

5 High School Cadets

Sousa

6 Blue Bells of Scotland

Fine

7 Variation (Duet Part)

D.C. al Fine

LESSON 4
Changing Keys

1 Go Tell Aunt Rhodie (in B♭)

2 Rhodie's Cousin (in E♭)

3 Rhodie's Second Cousin (in F)

4 Shifting Gears

5 St. Nick

6 Bill Grogan's Goats

Partner Songs

7 "Rueben 'n Rachel"

8 Row, Row, Row

B-378

Eighth, Quarter And Dotted-Quarter Rhythms

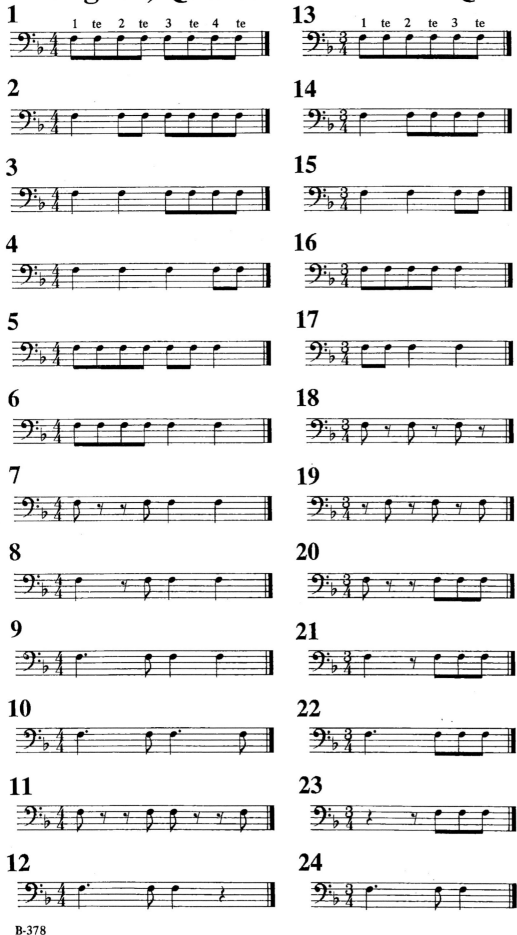
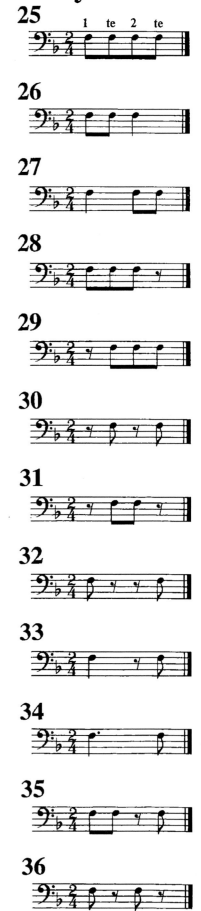

LESSON 5
The Dotted-Quarter-Note Lesson

1 Rhythmic Precision

2 Duet Part

3 Clarinets Help

4 Taps

5 Deck The Halls

6 All Through The Night

7 Dotted-Quarter Round

9

B-378

LESSON 6
More Dotted-Quarter Notes

1 **Stay Together Duo**

2 **Duet Part**

3 **Chromatic Exercise**

Watch Out!

4 **Men of Harlech**

5 **Auld Lang Syne**

6 **Minor Melody**

7 **Accomp.**

LESSON 7
The Syncopation Lesson

1 **Eighth Note Etude**

2 **Syn-Co-Pa Duo**

3 **Syncopated Chromatic**

Careful!

4 **Tom Dooley**

5 **Red River Valley**

6 **That's Where My Money Goes**

7 **You're A Grand Old Flag**

Cohan

LESSON 8
Harder Syncopation

1 Multiple Syncopation

2 Duet Part

3 Chromatic Syncopation - Watch Carefully!

4 Cindy

5 Old Gray Mare

6 John Henry

(Wait)

7 Hoky Poky

SIXTEENTH NOTE RHYTHMS

(To be played with 4 impulses per beat)

LESSON 9
Sixteenth Notes

(More 4 impulses per beat)

1 **Rhythmic Scale**

2 **Part Two**

3 **Echo Song**

4 **Part Two**

5 **Music In The Air**

6 **Polly Wolly Doodle**

7 **Round: Frere Jacques**

LESSON 10
(More 4 impulses per beat)

1 Rhythmic Challenge

2 Duet Part

3 Chromatic Scale

4 Mixed-Up Echo

5 Duet Part

6 Skip To My Lou

7 Up On The Housetop

8 Someone's In The Kitchen With Dinah

LESSON 11
The Enharmonic Lesson

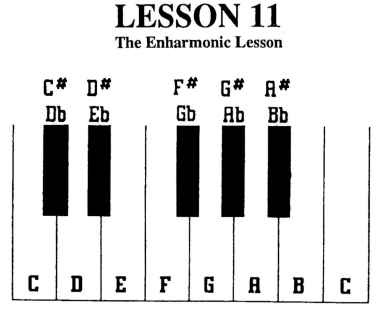

1 Enharmonic Echo

2 Echo Part

3 Ascending And Descending Chromatic Scales

4 Song With Accidentals

LESSON 12
The A-flat Concert Lesson

1 Our New Scale

2 Duet Part

3 Follow The Leader

4 Tutti

5 This Old Man

6 This New Man

7 American Patrol

Meacham

8 Accomp.

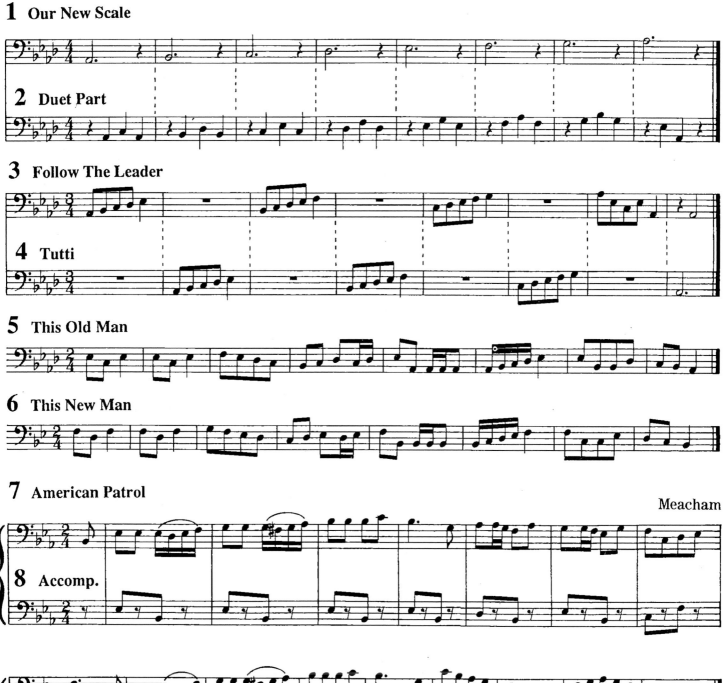

DOTTED EIGHTH AND SIXTEENTH RHYTHMS
(To be played with 4 impulses per beat)

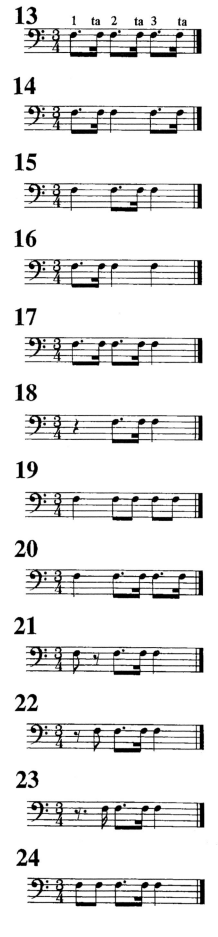

LESSON 13
Dotted-Eighth Lesson

1 Fun Dotted-Eighths

2 Duet Part

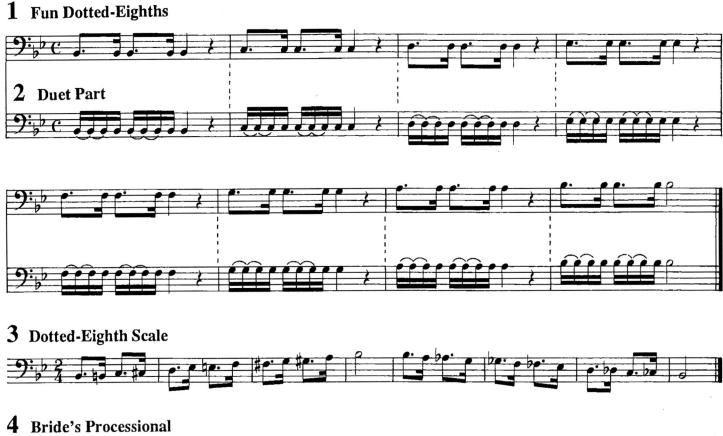

3 Dotted-Eighth Scale

4 Bride's Processional

5 O Christmas Tree

6 Processional

B-378

LESSON 14

1 **Rhythm Matching**

2 **Rhythm Matching Duet**

3 **Dotted Chromatic**

4 **Dotted-Eighth Processional**

5 **Duet Part**

6 **Rigoletto**

Verdi

7 **Texas Song**

8 **Humoresque** (Dvorak)

Partner Songs

9 **Swanee River** (Foster)

LESSON 15

1 Dotted Scale

2 Dotted Duo

3 Duet Part

4 Railroad Song

5 March Of The Kings

6 Santa Lucia

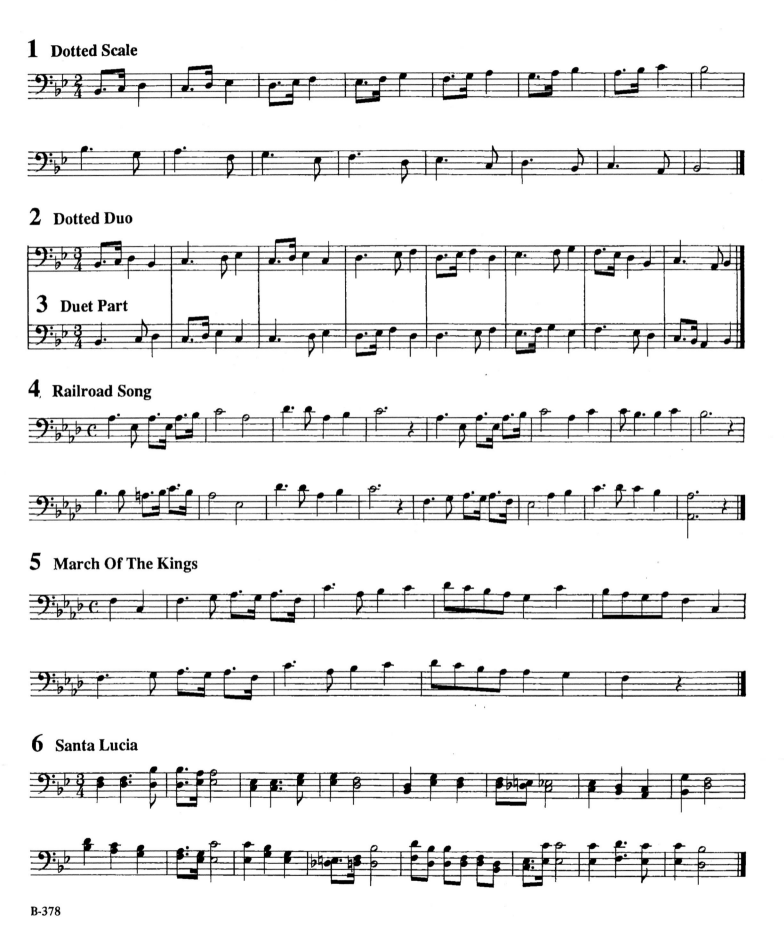

LESSON 16
More Of The Same

1 Concert D-flat Scale Rhythm Practice

2 Air

3 Andante Duet

4 Duet Part

COMPOUND TIME RHYTHMS

Remember — the foot tap is "down-press-up"

LESSON 17
The 3/8 Lesson

1 Scale With Arpeggios

2 Part 2

3 Chromatic Scale in 3/8

4 Back Down Again

5 Good Morning To You

6 Halloween Song

7 Walking Down The Street

LESSON 18
The 6/8 Lesson

1 **Scale Rhythms**

2 **Duet Part**

3 **Over The River And Through The Woods**

4 **Three Blind Mice (Round)**

5 **Man On The Flying Trapeze**

(In One)

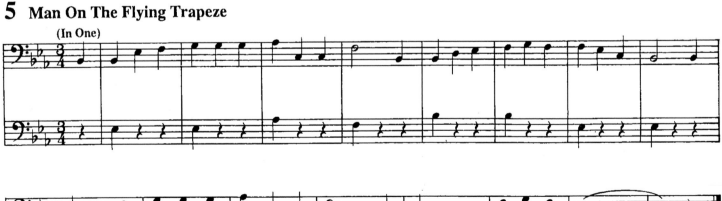

LESSON 19

1 **Chromatic Drill**

2 **Chromatic Speed Drill**

3 **For He's A Jolly Good Fellow**

4 **Drink To Me Only**

5 **Farmer In The Dell (Round)**

6 **Semper Fidelis**

Sousa

7 **Accomp.**

LESSON 20

1 Scale In 9/8

2 Scale In 12/8

3 Morning Song

4 Sorcerer's Apprentice *(What is the last note of the 1st measure?)* Dukas

5 The Last Song

SUPPLEMENTARY LESSON I

1 **Triplet Scale And Arpeggio**

2 **Chromatic Triplets**

3 **Etude**

4 **Beautiful Dreamer**

Foster

5 **Accomp.**

SUPPLEMENTARY LESSON II
(Extra Help To Get Ready For The Next Book)

1 lah lee   1 ta lah ta lee ta   1 lah ta lee ta   1 ta lee

1 Old Scale Rhythm

2 New Scale Rhythm

3 Etude

4 Happy Day

5 Greensleeves

6 Scheherazade Theme

B-378

Division of Beat

RHYTHM EXERCISES

Suggestion: For best results, use a metronome.

Set 1: The Blue and Green Slides

(All exercises on this page can be counted with 2 impulses)

*Exercises 73-84 should be counted one beat per measure using three pulses.
You could be tested on some of these rhythms.

RHYTHM EXERCISES
Set 2: The Green and Red Slides
(For 3 impulses and 4 impulses)

Suggestion: For best results, use a metronome.

B-378

Division of Beat

RHYTHM EXERCISES

Set 3: The Yellow Slides
(for 6 impulses)

*EASTMAN SYSTEM OF COUNTING (Simplified)
I. Notes of one or more counts

Notes of one count (or longer) are counted much the same way as any counting system; simply say the number of the count on which the note begins and continue the word-sound for the duration of the note. Thus a note which receives one count and which begins on the first beat of the measure would be counted "one"; if it were on the second count, say "two", etc. A note of longer value would simply be held longer; thus a whole note (in ¼ time) would be counted "onnnnnnnnnnne" for 4 counts. This has the advantage of making the verbalization most nearly approximate the sound of an instrument playing the actual rhythm and requires the identical mental process of thinking the number of counts while a continuous sound is produced. The following example quickly illustrates Eastman Counting as applied to rhythms (including rests) of 1, 2, 3 or 4 counts.

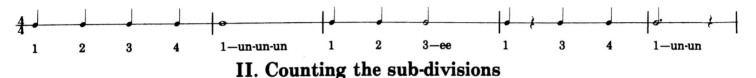

II. Counting the sub-divisions

Notes which receive less than a full count are divided into rhythms which are divisable by 2 and those which are divisable by 3 (some would say duple and triple rhythms). Again, any note which occurs on a downbeat is simply counted with the number of the count; the important difference is that a note which occurs the last ½ of a count is counted "te" (latin, rhymes with May) and notes which occur on the second ⅓ of the count and last ⅓ of the count are counted "lah" and "lee."

III. *Everything* else is counted "Ta"

IV. Unusual counting situations

1. Two-beat triplet

2. 32nd Notes

3. Triplets in sub-division

4. When a measure contains beats of unequal duration, such as ⅝ or ⅞. Those beats with extra eighth notes are considered to have an extra "Te."

*For the complete explanation of this counting system, see *Ear Training and Sight Singing Dictation Manual* by Alan I. McHose, published by Prentice Hall.

MUSICAL TERMS, ABBREVIATIONS AND SIGNS

Accelerando—accel.	Gradually faster
Adagio	Slowly
Ad libitum	At liberty
Allargando	Louder and slower
Allegretto	Moderately fast; slower than *allegro*
Andantino	Faster than *andante*
Animato	With animation; with life
A tempo	In the original tempo
Cantabile	In a song-like style
Chromatic	Proceeding by half tones
Coda	The ending
Con brio	With spirit
Con moto	With motion
Crescendo—cresc.	Gradually louder
Da Capo—D.C.	Return to the beginning
Dal Segno—D.S.	From the sign
Decrescendo—decresc.	Gradually softer
Diminuendo—dim.	Gradually diminish sound
Dolce	Sweetly
Fine	The end
Forte—f	Loud
Fortissimo—ff	Very loud
Forzando—fz	With sudden emphasis
Giocoso	Humorously; playfully
Largo	The slowest tempo mark
Legato	In a smooth, connected style
Leggiero	Light; swift
Lento	Slowly, between *andante* and *largo*
L'istesso	In the same time or tempo
Ma non troppo	But not too much
Marcato	Marked; accented
Marcia	In a march style
Meno mosso	Less motion; slower
Mezzo piano—mp	Moderately soft
Mezzo forte—mf	Moderately loud
Moderato	Moderately
Molto	Very much
Morendo	Dying away
Pianissimo—pp	Very soft
Piano—p	Softly
poco a poco	Little by little
Presto	Very quick; faster than *allegro*
Rallentando—rall.	Gradually slower
Ritardando—rit.	Retarding; holding back
Ritenuto	Retarding; holding back
Simile	In the same manner
Sforzando—sfz	With emphasis on a single note or chord
Solo	For one performer
Soli	For all
Staccato	Separated; disconnected
Tutti	All; together
Valse	Waltz
Vivace	Lively; sprightly
𝄋	Sign
⊕	to *Coda*
⫷	*Crescendo*
⫸	*Decrescendo*
>	Accent

Selected Trombone/ Euphonium Publications

SOLO WITH PIANO

BARAT, J.E.
SS361   Andante et Allegro   HL3773993

BARAT, J.E.
Smith, Glenn E.
SS974   Introduction and Dance   HL3774665

BELLSTEDT, HERMAN
Simon, Frank
SS371   Napoli   HL3774006

Napoli is perhaps the most famous solo by Sousa arranger and cornet virtuoso Hermann Bellstedt. Conceived as a theme and variations on a wildly popular 19th Century song, this edition by Bellstedt's student and Sousa band successor Frank Simon remains the one most performed today. This edition for trombone and euphonium by Tommy Fry comes with both bass and treble clef barts.

DAVIS, WILLIAM MAC
ST444   Variations on a Theme Of Robert Schumann   HL3775131
Concert band accompaniment also published by Southern Music. (S537CB)

EWAZEN, ERIC
SU450   Ballade for Bass or Tenor Trombone (reduction)   HL3776369
Ballade for Bass or Tenor Trombone is based on an earlier work for clarinet and string orchestra. This arrangement was written for Charles Vernon of the Chicago Symphony in 1996, who later recorded the work on Albany Records (Troy 479). Comes with separate bass and tenor trombone parts. Duration ca. 12'.

SU339   Concerto No. 1 for Trombone (Sonata for   HL3776236
         Trombone)
Completed in the Spring of 1993, Ewazen's Sonata for Trombone was commissioned by Michael Powell who premiered the work at the Aspen Music Festival and recorded it on Cala Records. Later orchestra and band arrangements followed, both of which feature an added cadenza and are available separately from the publisher. Duration ca. 18', Grade 5.

GAUBERT, PHILIPPE
SS167   Morceau Symphonique   HL3773773

HAACK, PAUL
ST381   Sweet Betsy Suite   HL3775046
An enjoyable and melodic set of variations on an American folk song. Contains both and treble clef and bass clef parts. And addition for trumpet also available from the publisher.

HANDEL, GEORGE FRIDERIC
Marsteller, Robert
SS464   Concerto in f Minor   HL3774088
Originally in G minor for oboe and chamber orchestra, this transcription for trombone is presented in F minor as a more practical key for the trombone. The custom of soloists of the Baroque Period to extemporize and embellish over a sustained line is preserved with an interpolated optional variation on the Sarabande. And and optional cadenza is included.

HANDEL, GEORGE FRIDERIC
Powell, Richard
SS827   Sonata No. 3   HL3774492
The only edition of this work that includes a Bb treble solo part for trumpet or euphonium in addition to the bass clef part. Originally for flute, this five movement sonata is an ideal recital piece; lengthy enough to be considered a major work, varied enough to prove the performer's ability in technique, sound, control, range and musicianship; yet not so difficult to be out of the range of the average high school trombonist.

HOFFMAN, EARL
ST100   Trigger Treat (bass trombone)   HL3774692

MARCELLO, BENEDETTO
Merriman, Lyle
SS806   Adagio and Allegro   HL3774474

SS807   Largo and Allegro   HL3774475

MOZART, WOLFGANG AMADEUS
Marsteller, Robert
ST94   Concerto in B-flat, K191 (B flat Major)   HL3775812
Transcribed by one of the great American trombonists of the 20th Century, Robert Marsteller, longtime player with the LA Philharmonic after World War II. This concerto, originally for bassoon, features delightful but challenging passages for the advanced trombonist.

MOZART, WOLFGANG AMADEUS
Powell, Richard
SS842   Arietta and Allegro, K109B/8 K3   HL3774509

NUX, PAUL VERONGE DE LA
SS145   Concert Piece   HL3773749
An andante-allegro work in a single movement edition inscribed for the National School Music Competition-Festivals.

SENAILLE, JEAN BAPTISTE
Falcone, Leonard
SS563   Allegro Spiritoso   HL3774203
This well known piece is arranged for baritone, euphonium, or trombone. Both bass clef and treble clef parts are provided.

SPEARS, JARED
ST311   Ritual and Celebration   HL3774957
The character of the "Ritual" movement is dramatic and slow, which trasitions without pause to the quick and lively "Celebration". Commissioned by and dedicated to Ken Kistner.

Exclusively distributed by  HAL•LEONARD® CORPORATION

Questions/ comments? info@laurenkeisermusic.com

Selected Trombone/ Euphonium Publications

METHODS

MARSTELLER, ROBERT

B268   Basic Routines   HL3770381

A volume of calisthenic exercises compiled to assist in the muscle development used in playing the trombone.Exercises are broken into four sections: (1)Attack and tome placement; (2) Slow Slurs; (3) Flexibility; (4) Scales and Arpeggios

COLLECTIONS

BACH, J.S.

Marsteller, Robert

B403   Six Suites, Bk. 1 (Suites 1, 2, 3)   HL3770615

The set of six Suites for Violoncello Solo is a monumental masterpiece of the Baroque Period. This edition for trombone, baritone or bassoon presents the Suites in their original keys. Optional notes for the use of the Bass Trombone, or any instrument with an "F" attachment, are noted.

BORDOGNI, GIULIO

Hoffman, Earl

B385   17 Vocalises   HL3770586

The vocalises by Marco Bordogni provide excellent practice material for trombone students. In order to make these melodious exercises even more interesting for both the student and the teacher, the arranger has composed second parts in contrapuntal form resulting in duets which are pleasing as well as practical. The added second part is generally somewhat more difficult than the original and may be considered to be the teacher's part. However, as the student progresses, they should master both parts. Theses pieces may also be performed by other like bass clef instruments.

SOLO WITH PIANO

BARAT, J.E.

SS361   Andante et Allegro   HL3773993

BARAT, J.E.

Smith, Glenn E.

SS974   Introduction and Dance   HL3774665

BELLSTEDT, HERMAN

Simon, Frank

SS371   Napoli   HL3774006

Napoli is perhaps the most famous solo by Sousa arranger and cornet virtuoso Herman Bellstedt. Conceived as a theme and variations on a wildly popular 19th Century song, this edition by Bellstedt's student and Sousa band successor Frank Simon remains the one most performed today. This edition for trombone and euphonium by Tommy Fry comes with both bass and treble clef barts.

DAVIS, WILLIAM MAC

ST444   Variations on a Theme Of Robert Schumann   HL3775131

Concert band accompaniment also published by Southern Music. (S537CB)

EWAZEN, ERIC

SU450   Ballade for Bass or Tenor Trombone (reduction)   HL3776369

Ballade for Bass or Tenor Trombone is based on an earlier work for clarinet and string orchestra. This arrangement was written for Charles Vernon of the Chicago Symphony in 1996, who later recorded the work on Albany Records (Troy 479). Comes with separate bass and tenor trombone parts. Duration ca. 12'.

SU339   Concerto No. 1 for Trombone (Sonata for Trombone)   HL3776236

Completed in the Spring of 1993, Ewazen's Sonata for Trombone was commissioned by Michael Powell who premiered the work at the Aspen Music Festival and recorded it on Cala Records. Later orchestra and band arrangements followed, both of which feature an added cadenza and are available separately from the publisher. Duration ca. 18', Grade 5.

HANDEL, GEORGE FRIDERIC

Powell, Richard

SS827   Sonata No. 3   HL3774492

The only edition of this work that includes a Bb treble solo part for trumpet or euphonium in addition to the bass clef part. Originally for flute, this five movement sonata is an ideal recital piece; lengthy enough to be considered a major work, varied enough to prove the performer's ability in technique, sound, control, range and musicianship; yet not so difficult to be out of the range of the average high school trombonist.

MARCELLO, BENEDETTO

Merriman, Lyle

SS806   Adagio and Allegro   HL3774474

SS807   Largo and Allegro   HL3774475

MOZART, WOLFGANG AMADEUS

Marsteller, Robert

ST94   Concerto in B-flat, K191 (B flat Major)   HL3775812

Transcribed by one of the great American trombonists of the 20th Century, Robert Marsteller, longtime player with the LA Philharmonic after World War II. This concerto, originally for bassoon, features delightful but challenging passages for the advanced trombonist.

MOZART, WOLFGANG AMADEUS

Powell, Richard

SS842   Arietta and Allegro, K109B/8 K3   HL3774509

NUX, PAUL VERONGE DE LA

SS145   Concert Piece   HL3773749

An andante-allegro work in a single movement edition inscribed for the National School Music Competition-Festivals.

SENAILLE, JEAN BAPTISTE

Falcone, Leonard

SS563   Allegro Spiritoso   HL3774203

The "Allegro Spiritoso" is the 3rd movement of a Sonata in D Minor. This well known piece is arranged for baritone, euphonium, or trombone. Both bass clef and treble clef parts are provided. Versions for following instruments are available from the publisher: alto clarinet, bass clarinet, contra alto clarinet, contrabass clarinet, alto saxophone, tenor saxophone, baritone saxophone, bassoon, euphonium/trombone, and tuba.

SPEARS, JARED

ST311   Ritual and Celebration   HL3774957

The character of the "Ritual" movement is dramatic and slow, which trasitions without pause to the quick and lively "Celebration". Commissioned by and dedicated to Ken Kistner.

TRIO

MENDELSSOHN, FELIX

Collins, Wilbur

ST350   Lift Thine Eyes   HL3775004

Exclusively distributed by  HAL•LEONARD® CORPORATION

Questions/ comments? info@laurenkeisermusic.com